Growing
Vegetable
Soup

Written and illustrated by
Lois Ehlert

SILVER BURDETT GI

Needham, MA   Parsippany, NJ
Atlanta, GA   Deerfield, IL   Irving, TX   Sant

DEDICATED TO MY FELLOW GARDENERS:
GLADYS, HARRY, JOHN, AND JAN

 SILVER BURDETT GINN
A Division of Simon & Schuster
160 Gould Street
Needham Heights, MA 02194–2310

GROWING VEGETABLE SOUP

Simon & Schuster edition, 1996

3 4 5 6 7 8 9 10 BA 01 00 99 98 97

ISBN: SSB 0–663–60235–1
       BSB 0–663–60220–3

Dad says we are going to grow vegetable soup.

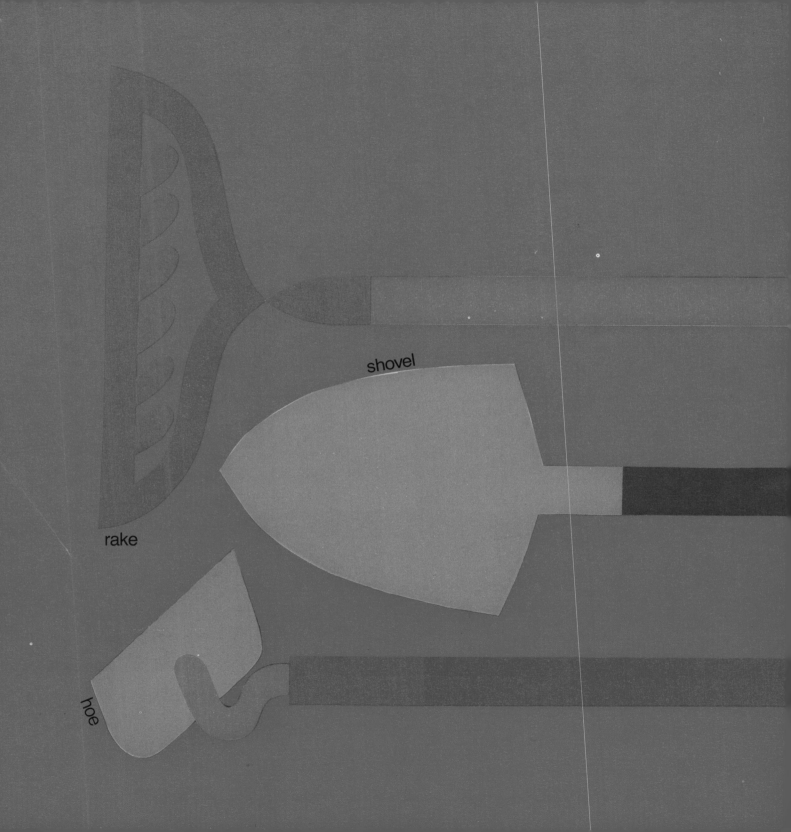

rake

shovel

hoe

4

We're ready to work, and our tools are ready, too.

We are planting

seed package

soil

hole

the seeds,

garden glove

green bean
seed

pea
seed

corn
seed

zucchini squash
seed

carrot
seeds

and all the sprouts,

broccoli

TOMATO

potato eyes

trowel

set onions

PEPPER

CABBAGE

peat moss pot

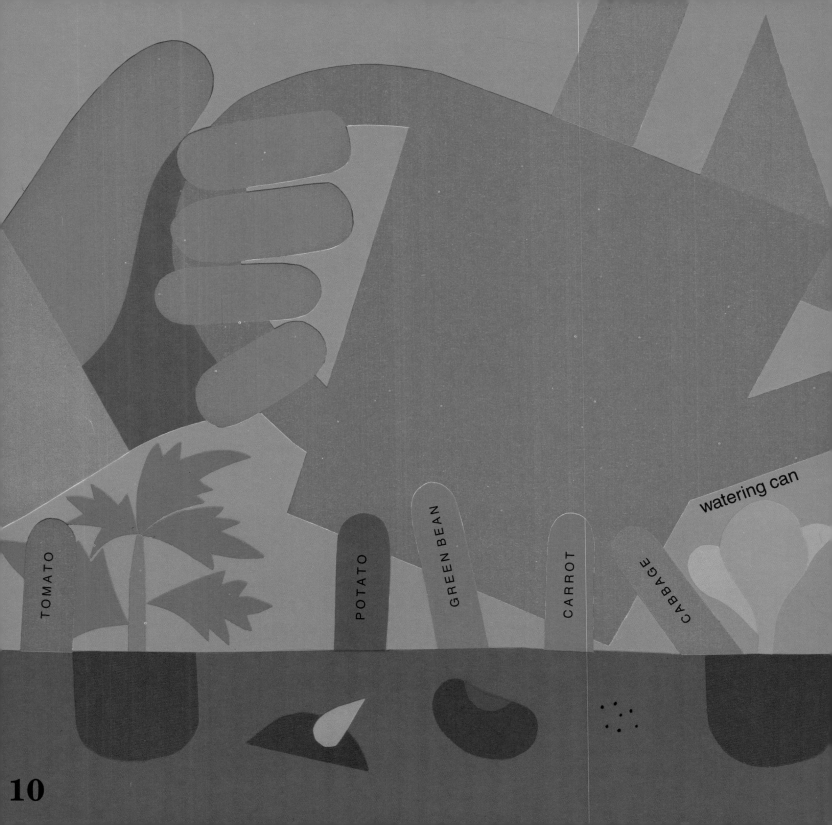

TOMATO

POTATO

GREEN BEAN

CARROT

CABBAGE

watering can

10

and giving them water,

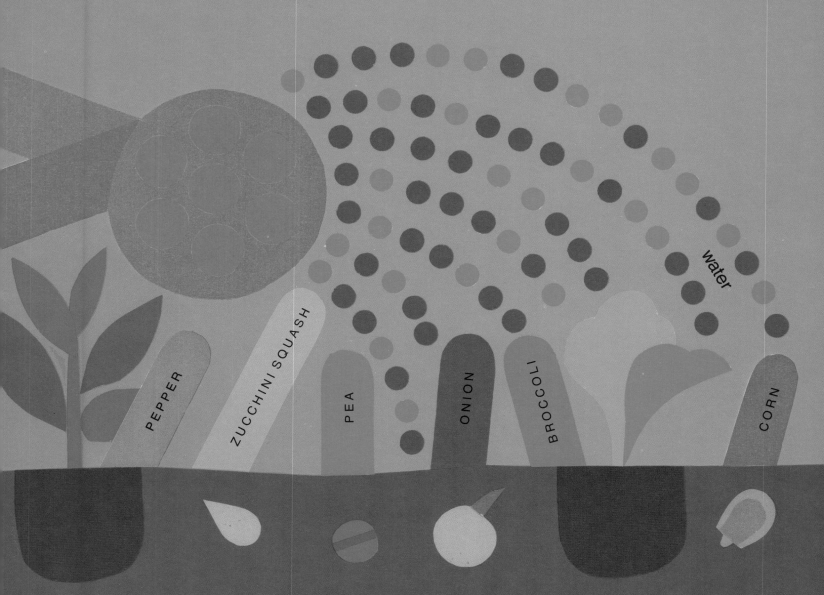

11

and waiting for warm sun to make them grow,

12

13

and grow,

soil

ZUCCHINI SQUASH

ONION

POTATO

PEA

CARROT

CORN

weed

SUN

PEPPER

TOMATO

CABBAGE

GREEN BEAN

BROCCOLI

15

and grow into plants.

squash
bud

squash
blossom

ZUCCHINI SQUASH

17

We watch

worm

BROCCOLI

18

over them and weed,

hand
grubber

GREEN BEAN

until the vegetables
are ready for us
to pick

TOMATO

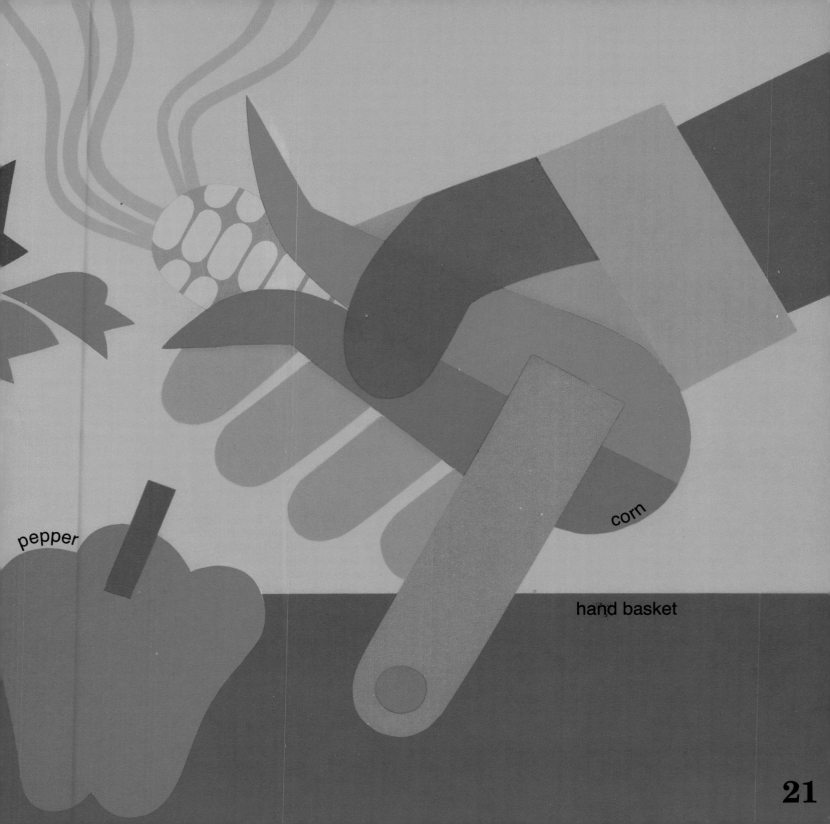

pepper

corn

hand basket

21

spading
fork

22

or dig up

carrot

potato

bushel basket

and carry home.
Then we wash them

cabbage

onion

pail

and cut them and put them in a pot of water,

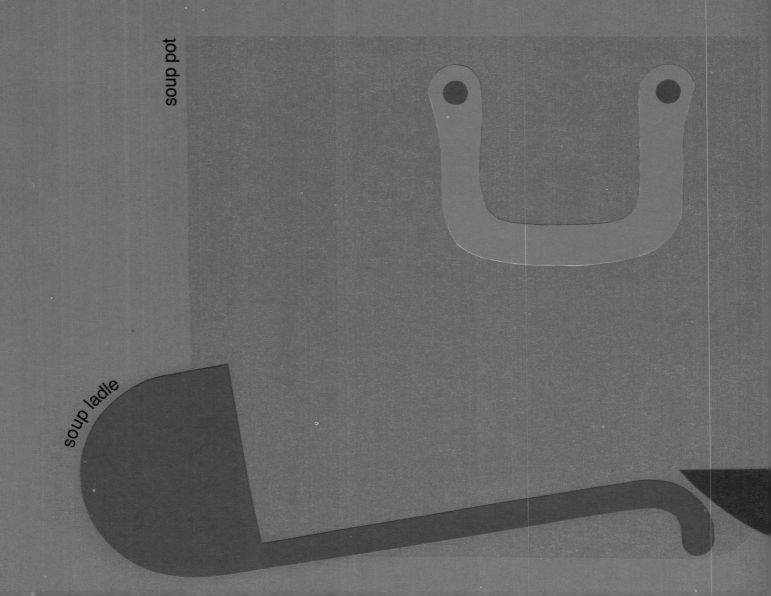

soup pot

soup ladle

carrot

corn

onion

zucchini squash

tomato

pea

broccoli

potato

pepper

green bean

knife

cabbage

27

and cook them into vegetable soup!

steam

29

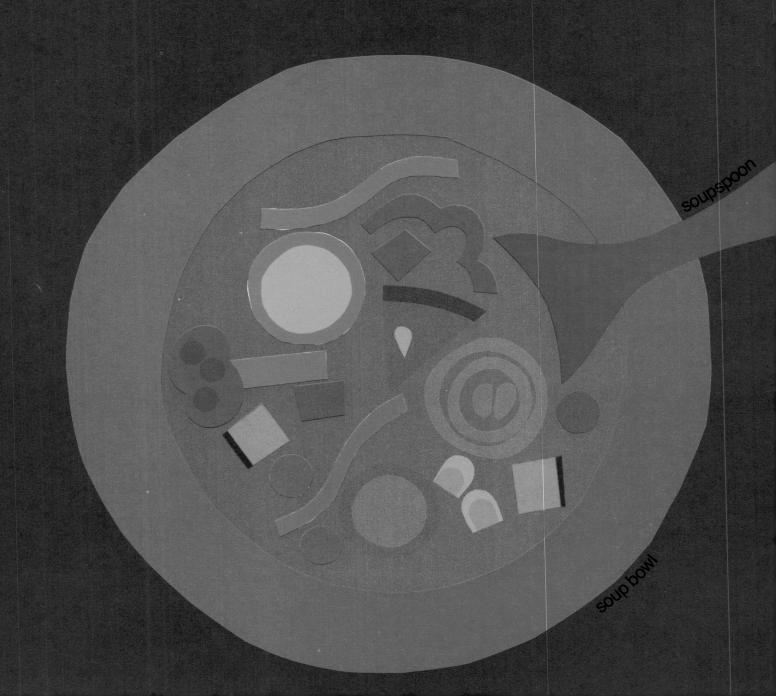

soupspoon

soup bowl

30

At last it's time
to eat it all up!

It was the
best soup ever...

and we can
grow it again
next year.